Why Must I...

Exercise?

Jackie Gaff

Photography by Chris Fairclough

CHERRYTREE BOOKS

ISBN 1-84234-348-3

Planned and produced by Discovery Books Ltd.
Editor: Helena Attlee
Designers: Ian Winton and Rob Norridge
Illustrator: Joanna Williams
Consultant: Pat Jackson, Professional Officer for School Nursing, The Community Practitioners' and
Health Visitors' Association.

Acknowledgments
The author and publisher would like to thank the following for kind permission to reproduce photographs:
Corbis: page 4 (Michael S. Yamashita), page 5 (Ariel Skelley), page 9 (Joyce Choo), page14 (Gabe
Palmer), page 15 (Jose Luis Pelaez, inc./Corbis), page16 (Ron Morsch), page 19 (Ariel Skelley), page 27
(Jose Luis Pelaez, inc./Corbis), page 25 (Troy Wayrynen/New Sport/Corbis); Getty Images: page 7 (Taxi),
page 28 (Stone).
Commissioned photography by Chris Fairclough.

The author, packager, and publisher would like to thank the following people for their participation in
the book: Alice Baldwin-Hay, Heather and William Cooper and Ieuan Crowe.

Contents

Why Must I Exercise?

Exercise is fun. It keeps your body fit and strong, and it can make you feel more cheerful.

If you don't exercise your body will become out of shape, and everything will start to feel like hard work.

Computer games are great — but don't spend all day playing them.

Staying in shape will make your body strong enough to do everything it was designed to do.

4

When you are in shape you can easily run for a bus, pedal your bike up a steep hill, or race down the football field to score a touchdown.

Getting fit now will make your heart and lungs strong. It will help to keep you healthy for the rest of your life.

HEALTHY HINTS

- **Ask your parent or guardian if they will walk or bike to school with you.**

- **Try out a new sport or game.**

- **Do something active every day.**

Try to find a sport that suits you. There is something for everyone.

So keep your body happy — switch off that computer and get moving!

All Sorts of Exercise

Lots of different things count as exercise, so find something you enjoy.

Here are some ideas for exercising: kick a ball around, fly a kite, take the dog for a walk, or put on a favorite CD and dance around your bedroom.

Dogs need exercise every day – and so do you!

Dancing can be a great way to get fit. It makes you more flexible and graceful, too.

HEALTHY HINTS

- Always play somewhere safe — in the yard, or with your friends in the park.

Why not join a **martial arts** class, or start a football or tennis club? It's a great way to make new friends.

Playing tennis will make your arms strong and speed up your **reactions**.

7

Mighty Muscles

Your muscles give you the strength to move. Without them you couldn't even blink your eyes.

Muscles do their job by pulling on bones, skin, or other body parts. They tighten to pull, and **relax** to let go.

Muscles can only pull, not push, so they have to work together to get things done.

Mighty mouse

The Romans thought that muscles looked like mice running around under the skin, so they called them *musculi*, or "little mice." Over the years, the Romans' *musculi* became our word muscles.

When you smile, 15 different muscles get to work.

8

When you bend your arm, your **biceps** pulls your forearm toward your shoulder.

When you straighten your arm, another big muscle called the **triceps** pulls it back down again.

Some muscles work in pairs, while others work in teams.

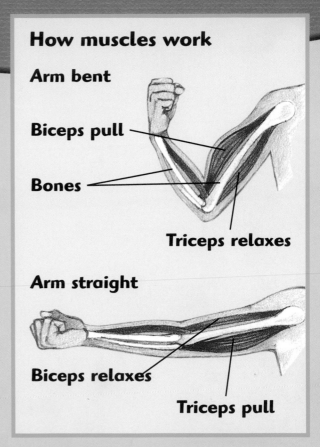

How muscles work

Arm bent

Biceps pull

Bones

Triceps relaxes

Arm straight

Biceps relaxes

Triceps pull

For example, about 200 muscles team up every time you take a step.

When you climb a rope the muscles in your arms and legs work hard to pull your body upward.

Warming Up

You must prepare your body for exercise by warming up your muscles.

Warm muscles are more **flexible**, so they are easier to stretch. This makes your body more flexible all over.

Muscles can be damaged if they are overworked before they are ready. This is called a **strain**, and it makes the muscle sore to touch and painful to use.

Warm up the muscles at the top of your back by stretching both arms out in front of you, with knuckles facing outward. Press outward. Do this five times.

Loosen your shoulder muscles by circling your arms, one at a time. Work for a minute on each side.

- **Always do some gentle warm ups before you do any serious exercise.**

Jogging gently on the spot for three minutes is a good way to warm up your muscles.

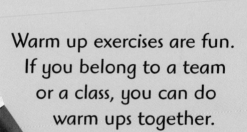

Warm up exercises are fun. If you belong to a team or a class, you can do warm ups together.

Take hold of your left foot and lift it up, while pressing your hip forward. Repeat on the other side to warm up the thigh muscles in both legs. Do this five times.

Stretching exercises make your body more flexible. This means that you can bend your body more easily.

Try sitting on the floor with your legs stretched straight out in front of you. Can you touch your toes? If not, you should do exercises that help your **joints** to bend easily.

A flexible body is much more graceful than a stiff one. Ballet dancers are very flexible, and so are gymnasts.

Stretching exercises help your muscles to lengthen and relax. This means that they become more flexible.

Try these exercises:

1. On all fours, pull your head and bottom together, so that your back is rounded.

2. Now raise your head and hips, so that you are stretching your body in the opposite direction.

3. Now kneel upright and push your hips down, toward your heels. Stretch your arms in front of you.

HEALTHY HINTS

- Get into the habit of stretching:
- Stretch when you get up in the morning.
- Stretch after you have been sitting down.
- Stretch while you are watching television.
- Stretch while you are sitting at the computer.
- Stretch when you are lying in bed.

Tower of Strength

Exercise won't give you any new muscles, but working muscles a little harder will build up their strength.

Tennis is a great way to strengthen your arm muscles. Riding your bike will make your leg muscles stronger, and so will cross-country running.

Ice-skating makes your leg muscles stronger.

There are lots of different ways to strengthen your arm muscles.

HEALTHY HINTS

- **If you feel weak or dizzy while you exercise, stop and rest.**

- **Don't punish your body by over-exercising.**

Exercising your muscles is also good for your bones. When muscles move, they put **pressure** on the bones. This pressure makes the bones grow thicker and stronger.

Yoga exercises your muscles and makes your whole body more flexible.

15

Teaming up

Soccer, basketball, and football are all team games — they are a great way of exercising.

If you don't enjoy the team games you play at school, try something else. What about field hockey or volleyball? Find out about new games. There's sure to be something you really enjoy.

As well as helping you to exercise, team games teach you to work with other people.

Ancient Soccer

Soccer was first played in China, about 2,300 years ago. You had to keep the ball in the air, not kick it along the ground!

Whatever game you choose, you will need **stamina** to succeed. Stamina is the strength that keeps you going, allowing you to play your best to the very end of the game. The more you exercise, the more stamina you will build up.

Going Solo

If team games aren't for you, don't let that stop you from exercising.

If you like doing your own thing, but you also want to meet people, why not join a class or club?

If you live close to a lake, a river, or even a swimming pool, you might be able to join a canoe or kayak club.

Ballet develops your muscle-strength and **coordination.**

Paddling a kayak is exciting, and it strengthens your arm, shoulder, and chest muscles.

HEALTHY HINTS

- Wear comfortable clothes when you exercise.

- Take an extra layer to put on afterward.

- Never use a trampoline or go near water without a grownup.

Try to find out about local sports clubs. Gym classes are an excellent way to exercise.

Gymnastics improves your balance, your strength, and your overall flexibility.

Taking a Deep Breath

Whether you're running for a train or racing up and down a swimming pool, hard exercise takes a lot of energy.

Your body gets its energy from the food you eat, but it needs a gas called oxygen to release the energy in the food.

The blood supply

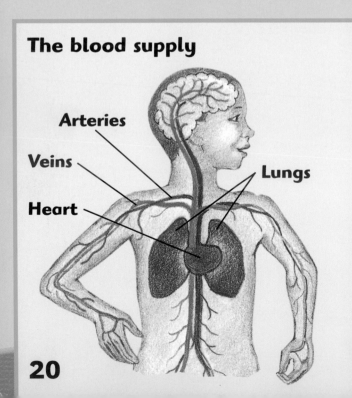

Arteries

Veins

Lungs

Heart

Oxygen is in the air that you breathe into your lungs. It is carried away from your lungs by your blood. The heart muscle pumps this blood all around your body.

This picture shows the blood supply. The arteries carry blood away from the heart, and the veins carry it back to the heart again.

Activities that make your heart and lungs work harder are called **aerobic exercises.**

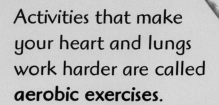

The more you exercise your lungs, the more air they can pull into your body, and the more exercise you can do

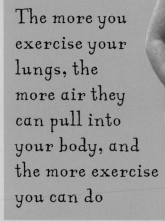

Your heart gets stronger and healthier with exercise. This means that you are less likely to have problems with your heart when you are older.

When you jump rope you exercise your heart, as well as your shoulders, arms and legs.

HEALTHY HINTS

- **Try to do some form of aerobic exercise two or three times a week, for twenty to thirty minutes at a time.**

Food and Fitness

It's no good doing lots of exercise unless you look after your body in other ways also.

Your body can't stay in shape from exercise alone. You need to eat healthy food, too.

Try to avoid food that contains lots of fat, salt, or sugar.

After you eat a meal, you should wait at least two hours before starting your exercises. Exercising too soon may give you a **cramp**.

HEALTHY HINTS

- **Sugary foods give you instant energy, but they can make you feel more tired later on.**

- **Take a bottle of water with you.**

- **Drink while you are exercising if you feel thirsty.**

It is important to eat as soon as you can after exercise, but it's no good following up your exercise with a lot of unhealthy, fatty food! A banana sandwich makes an ideal snack.

Sweating during exercise will make you feel very thirsty. Make sure you drink plenty of water, especially if the weather is hot.

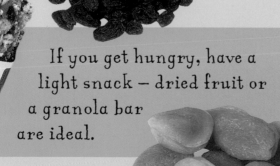

If you get hungry, have a light snack – dried fruit or a granola bar are ideal.

Cooling Down

Giving your body time to cool down is just as important as allowing it time to warm up.

Cool-down exercises let your body **temperature, heartbeat,** and **breathing rate** slowly get back to normal. They stop you from feeling stiff the next day.

Try to stretch all the muscles that you have been using. Make your movements gradually more gentle.

Stopping exercise too suddenly can send your body into shock. You'll get cold and shivery if you cool down too quickly. You may even feel dizzy and light-headed.

You are bound to feel hot when you finish exercising, but don't forget to put on an extra layer of clothes.

HEALTHY HINTS

- **Spend at least five minutes on your cool-downs.**

- **Put on more clothes so you don't get cold too quickly.**

- **Drink plenty of water after you have finished exercising.**

Athletes always put on a tracksuit after an event.

Exercise should make you feel good, not sick, so give your body a break — treat it to some cool-downs!

Five minutes spent on gentle cool-downs will stop you from feeling stiff later.

Getting Your Sleep

When you do lots of exercise, your body will need a good long rest each night.

All your muscles take it easy when you sleep, and your heartbeat and breathing rate slow down. Give your body time to wind down before bedtime.

Reading a book at bedtime will help you relax and drop off to sleep easily.

Try to go to bed at the same time each night. Your body loves this kind of **routine**.

Sleep is when your body builds up a fresh store of energy. If you wake up feeling tired or cross, you're probably not getting enough sleep!

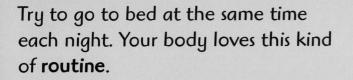

HEALTHY HINTS

- **Make sure you get at least eight hours' sleep each night.**

Stay Fit, Stay Happy

Do you feel tired and lacking in energy some days? Doing nothing won't help!

Exercise really can make you feel better. That's because it kick-starts your body into producing special **chemicals** that make you feel happier.

Sometimes it's easier to exercise with friends.

Exercising and eating healthily are two key steps on the road to a lifetime of feeling fit, happy, and fizzing with energy!

HEALTHY HINTS

- **Make the most of any games you play at school.**
- **Have fun in your free time — do activities you enjoy.**
- **Do not spend too much time sitting in front of a computer or television.**

Glossary

Aerobic exercises
Aerobic exercises are activities that make the heart and lungs work harder to get more oxygen pumping around the body.

Artery
A tube carrying blood from the heart to other parts of the body.

Biceps
The large muscle at the front of your upper arm.

Breathing rate
The speed at which you breathe, pulling air in and out of your lungs.

Chemicals
Chemicals are the substances that make up the world's materials.

Coordination
Ability to make controlled and graceful movements.

Cramp
Cramp is when a muscle goes tight and hard, and really hurts!

Flexible
Flexible means bending easily. Flexible people find it easy to touch their toes, for instance.

Heartbeat
Your heart is a muscle, and like all muscles it moves by tightening and relaxing — this is called its beat, or pulse.

Joint
Joints are places where two bones meet. Some are fixed, but others move — your elbows and knees have moveable joints, for example.

Martial arts
Judo, karate, t'ai chi, and tae kwon do are all martial arts, or sports that first grew up in Asia.

Pressure
Pressure is a pushing force.

Reaction
If you have fast reactions, it means that you move or respond quickly to different situations.

Relax
When a muscle relaxes, it softens and lets go.

Routine
A routine is a regular or set way of doing things.

Stamina
Stamina is another word for staying power — having the energy to keep on exercising, for example.

Strain
A strain is an injury caused by overworking the muscles.

Temperature
A measure of how hot or cold something is.

Triceps
The large muscle at the back of your upper arm.

Veins
A tube carrying blood from the body back to the heart.

Further Resources

Web Sites

www.kidshealth.org
A child-centered site devoted to all aspects of health and well-being. Includes advice on many different aspects of health and exercise.

www.noahhealth.org
A question-and-answer type site, devoted to all aspects of physical fitness for children.

www.bbc.co.uk/health
BBC web site containing articles and news on all aspects of child and adult health.

www.canandianparents.com
A lively web site covering all aspects of family life, including health and hygiene.

www.everybody.co.nz
New Zealand's health information web site.

Books

Brunhoff, Laurent de. *Barbar's Yoga for Elephants*. Harry N. Abrams Inc., 2002.

Ganeri, Anita. *Body Books – Get a Move On*. Evans, 2003.

Lobb, Janice. *Bump! Thump! How Do We Jump?* Kingfisher, 2000.

Byl, John. *101 Fun Warm-up and Cool-down Games*. Human Kinetics Publishers, 2004.

Royston, Angela. *Look After Yourself: Get Some Exercise*. Heinemann Library, 2003.

Royston, Angela. *My Amazing Body: Staying Healthy*. Raintree, 2004.

Index